November 4, 1978

Dear Na,

May you age appropriately, become of age while enjoying the wondrous World of Braces! I would love to give you one of each — and I will, as soon as you have the room. Tell the Queen Snow "Happy Birthday" (& her nose as well) for I have been thinking of her face. Notice the picture of your step sons, Henry and Sam. Love to you always)

Cher

The wondrous world of DOGS

Text by David Gibbon

Produced by Ted Smart

Photography © Colour Library International Ltd.

First published in Great Britain in 1976
by Colour Library International Ltd.

Printed by OFSA Milano and bound by L.E.G.O. Vicenza Italy

Display and text filmsetting by
Focus Photoset Ltd.,
134 Clerkenwell Road, London EC1R 5DL.

ISBN 0 8148 0667 8

Enquiries should be sent to:
Leon Amiel Publisher
31, W. 46th Street
New York
New York 10036

Henry Montefusco

Many books have been written about dogs. Some have been in the nature of learned treatise on all aspects of the whole vast subject; others have examined specific breeds, the behaviour of one particular type of dog, etc. In many instances authors have concentrated entirely on one aspect of the subject. There have even been whole books dealing just as thoroughly with one particular breed of dog. Books of collected poems about dogs have been published, and many famous persons have written of their own particular pets. Many have been written about wars dogs, many tales about working dogs, about Royal dogs, Presidential dogs and film stars dogs.

Looking back on conversations that have taken place through the years with innumerable people it occurred to me that I had met very few people indeed who did not have some sort of story to tell about a dog they had owned or knew of. If they had no story of their own to tell, then they certainly knew someone else who had. Very occasionally these stories concerned less than happy incidents but the vast majority were quite the reverse; stories of great intelligence shown by dogs, of great bravery and loyalty, devotion and understanding. Above all it seemed to me that the one outstanding feature that invariably emerged was the sheer friendliness of dogs towards man. It is this particular aspect of man's relationship with dogs, the friendship, that this book seeks to underline. It does not instruct, or even advise, on the management of dogs, but lets the dogs speak for themselves, largely in the form of the best pictures that could be assembled of the most appealing dogs that could be found. Hopefully the book will succeed in this respect at

(LEFT)
Old English Sheepdog.

(ABOVE)
Despite not having a pedigree, a very alert and attractive looking dog, and obviously a great companion.

least, although it is readily acknowledged that there may be, in some cases, more perfect examples of one particular breed or another. If so then the blame lies with us and not the dogs for we, it is to be earnestly hoped, no longer judge people by their breeding alone, and a dog can no more help what it is, or what it looks like, than any other creature on earth, man included! To every Mother her own child is, or should be, beautiful and the ugliest dog you could wish to see is no doubt as much loved by its owner as the latest bemedalled champion. This seems to me the right and proper way to regard these animals that have befriended man, and have thrown in their lot with him, for better or worse, since man first became the dominant species.

Although the origins of the relationship between man and dog go so far back in time the most surprising thing about it, to me at least, is that it should have endured for so long and still show no sign of diminishing–quite the reverse in fact. Man never seems to have grown tired of the companionship of dogs, and dogs, for their part, have remained ever faithful. It would seem reasonable to assume that, in the beginning, this relationship was formed out of common predatory instincts; the hunting and killing of other animals in order to provide food for survival. No doubt the companionship followed later. That this companionship developed into a real friendship is beyond question. There are too many instances of dogs risking, and indeed giving, their lives in order to save the life of a beloved

(ABOVE LEFT)
Great Dane. If you take out a Great Dane, it might well be a question of 'who takes who for a walk' for it is indeed a big dog. For many years they have been used as hunting and fighting dogs but, in fact, they can be very affectionate. Feeding and exercising such a large dog is not, however, something that should be taken on lightly!

(LEFT)
Spitz. The Spitz family includes the Keeshond, Elkhound and Samoyed. They are identified with Northern Scandinavia where they are used as hunting dogs and watch dogs.

(RIGHT)
Shetland Sheep Dogs.

← Ho ?

master or mistress. Certainly in many cases such dogs were not trained to do such a thing but did it quite instinctively. In the same way there have been many cases of men risking their lives in order to save that of a dog. If they do nothing else, at least these incidents serve to illustrate the depths of feeling and the deep bonds of loyalty that exist between some men and some dogs.

This, of course, is the serious side of the continuing relationship. There is another side, namely the sheer exuberance and joy that may be seen in a happy dog with its loving master or mistress. This happiness is surely epitomised by the sight of a young boy or girl with a dog, playing together as though energy was a bottomless well and tiredness something they had never heard of! Dogs undoubtedly adapt themselves to the requirements or abilities of their owners in a quite remarkable way. Not long ago I watched an elderly man, who obviously had great difficulty walking, struggling up a steep road in a little village in Devon. His dog, which I assumed to be equally old, plodded along with similar difficulty at his heels. We exchanged a few words and I was surprised to learn that, in fact, the dog was relatively young. I was told by the old man that, as he had become progressively more crippled over the last two or three years and had found it harder and harder to walk, so the dog had taken to walking more slowly, as though he was in some way expressing his sympathy and wanted to share his masters burden. I contrasted this particular relationship with that of my twelve year old daughter and 'Farthing', her beloved little Yorkshire terrier. Because of his small size he is singularly ill-equipped to keep up with her bounding energy – yet he does – and he will follow her over huge boulders on the sea-shore for hours on end, just to be with her. He would, I have no doubt, follow her to the ends of the earth if she wished to go there!

(LEFT)
Basset Hound.

(RIGHT)
Although a cross bred Setter, and therefore not eligible for a pedigree, this lovely dog has great appeal and a quiet dignity in its own right.

Sam
Montefusco

Mentioning my daughter and her dog reminds me of something that happened about four years ago that well illustrates how common ownership of dogs can bridge great gulfs in almost every respect. My daughter asked me one day, in the way that children do, if I knew how many dogs the Queen owned and if I knew their names. I told her that I believed the Queen had several Corgis but that I had no idea of their names. Again, in the way that children do, she said that perhaps she would write and ask her. I explained that the Queen was probably very busy and that I thought it unlikely that she would be able to find time to answer her. Undaunted, she sat down and wrote to the Queen that evening, telling her about her own dog and enquiring about Her Majesty's corgis, and particularly their names! The end of the story will be obvious by now for, sure enough, a few days later a letter dropped through the letter box, bearing no stamp, and addressed to Andrea. It had not occurred to me, until that moment, that of course the Queen would not require to have stamps put on her letters! Inside the envelope was a sheet of notepaper, headed by the Royal Crest, bearing the following: "Dear Andrea, I am commanded by the Queen to thank you for your letter, and to tell you in answer to your query that Her Majesty has four pet dogs which are all Corgis and whose names are Heather, Buzz, Tiny and Brush".

The vast majority of dogs are, of course, kept simply as pets by their owners. It is surprising, however, that in this day and age there are so many different ways in which they can still be of great service to man. The most obvious and, to my mind, certainly the most romantic, though I doubt if many of them would agree with me, is the shepherd working in close co-operation and understanding with his sheep dog and, seemingly without effort, controlling a flock of sheep to perfection. I'm quite sure that there

is really nothing romantic about it at all, and that it is sheer hard work, but there is an almost poetic quality in their obvious mastery of their craft, that has a great fascination for most people.

No doubt technology will, one day, make the use of guide dogs for the blind a thing of the past. If it makes the difficult life of blind people more comfortable and easier then this would, obviously, be all to the good. Until such a breakthrough happens, however, there will be many such people who will continue to find their dogs not only of great value to them in their everyday lives but will also feel that they have a constant companion by their side whose primary concern is their welfare.

Dogs will always, to the best of their ability, guard what they consider to be their home or their territory against intruders. This natural trait has been put to good use through the years in the training of guard dogs and, despite all the sophisticated methods that are now available, they are still heavily relied on for the protection of property. Without any form of training at all though, there are many people, particularly those who are living alone, who sleep more peacefully in the knowledge that they have a dog in the house.

Both the armed forces and the police still use dogs extensively and, I understand, there are dogs used for finding narcotics and explosives in much the same way as they are used to detect the presence of truffles; which no doubt earns them the gratitude of a great number of law-enforcement agencies on the one hand, and a great number of gourmets on the other!

At this particular time in the world's history there is, as we all know, a great shortage of many kinds of food. In addition to many other factors the problem of the world's dog population and its feeding has, not altogether surprisingly, been put forward as one of the many reasons for this present shortage. Whatever

(TOP LEFT)
Alsatian

(BOTTOM LEFT)
West Highland White Terrier

(RIGHT)
Old English Sheepdog.

may be the rights and wrongs of this argument most people who are concerned about either this rising population of dogs or, indeed, about their welfare, must surely agree about one thing; the altogether too easy way in which dogs can be obtained. The fact that a puppy, of almost any breed that can be imagined, is so appealing leads, inevitably, to an awful lot of impulse buying, particularly at such times as Christmas. All too often, it seems, the decision to be a dog owner lasts for only as long as the holidays and then, as soon as it is found that there is more to dog ownership than simply cuddling a warm puppy, the wretched creatures find themselves either turned out on the street or, worse still, dumped many miles away, to join the ranks of strays. Quite what the answer to this would be I wouldn't know, or perhaps it is that there are so many answers that it is difficult to sort out the practical from the impractical. It would seem, however,

(LEFT)
Labrador Retriever and pups

(ABOVE)
Spaniels

(RIGHT)
Alsatians

that certain minimum requirements should be imposed on both the buyers and sellers of dogs to try to prevent, to some extent, this unhappy state of affairs.

When I began this introduction I mentioned that almost everyone I met had a favourite story to tell concerning a dog. Perhaps not surprisingly, considering I have valued the companionship of dogs since I was a small child, I have a few memories of my own. There always seemed to be dogs around me when I was young and I naturally loved them all, but only once did I feel that I had a dog that truly belonged to me.

Many years ago, it seems like either a lifetime or only yesterday, so much has passed and very firmly etched in my mind is the memory. I had a dog called Ben. It was during the war and I was living with my Mother, in a small, almost deserted seaside town on the Yorkshire coast. I must have

John D'

been January and it was one of those bitterly cold winters when the snow was deep, the frost was hard and nightly, and the wind would seem to cut right through everything. It seemed colder, perhaps, because there were so few people around and, certainly, the only place to be was inside, in front of a warm fire. Quite why I, a twelve years old boy, was outside I don't recall, but I was coming back from somewhere and had almost reached the garden gate when I saw a big, almost shapeless, old dog walking painfully along in the middle of the road towards me. Even at night I could see that he was in a dreadful state, unkempt, visibly limping, and with all the appearance of having just about reached the limit of his

(RIGHT AND TOP LEFT)
Alsatians

(BELOW)
Corgis

(TOP LEFT)
Bulldogs

endurance. As he grew nearer I thought I recognised him as an Old English Sheepdog, although he was in such a sorry state that it was not easy to tell. Beyond our house there was nothing but a park and then the cliffs and the sea, and I remember wondering where he could be going. As I said, it was a small town and there were very few people living in it, and I was quite sure that I had never seen this particular dog before. As he drew nearer I spoke to him. He walked very slowly up to me and just stood looking at me. From that moment he hardly left my side until, nearly two years later. At first we just took him in for the night because we thought he would die if he was left out in that weather but when we got him inside and looked at his ice-encrusted feet

(TOP RIGHT)
Corgi

(BOTTOM)
Bloodhound

Stewardi

← *(a striking resemblance to Dory and Lisa)*

and his matted coat I asked if he could stay, if we could make him well again. We sat and bathed his feet and then, somehow, got him upstairs and into a bath. He offered no protest and seemed to assume that we were doing our best to help him. Gradually, over the weeks that passed, he recovered and the Spring came. No-one ever claimed him or seemed to know anything about him, and his appearance remained a mystery, but he became my dog and I called him Ben. There was never any doubt that he was my dog. He followed me everywhere I went, sometimes with great difficulty, for he was very old even then. My

(LEFT)
English Setter.

(ABOVE)
Bulldog. The first name that springs to mind when thinking of British dogs must surely be that of the Bulldog. Although once used for bull baiting it is a very good natured and affectionate dog. It seems to have suffered rather badly at the hands of breeders and its nose is now so short that even breathing is difficult.

(RIGHT)
Saluki or Gazelle dogs. Members of the Gazehound family, so called because they see rather than scent their prey. The Saluki can trace its ancestry back over five thousand years. It originated in Arabia where it was used as a hunting dog. It was introduced into Britain in the nineteenth century.

friends accepted him without question and, when we climbed fences that he could not, he would wait patiently while we struggled to lift him over. He was a big dog, and very wide. So wide in fact that we once discovered him in the pantry, which was very small, and he was too wide to turn round and come out. Eventually he backed out with an innocent look on his face and cream cake plastered all over it! When he eventually died, as I knew he must, I used to console myself with the thought that, whatever the rest of his life had been

like, at the very least the last two years had been happy, and he had returned in full measure, as nearly all dogs do, the affection he had been shown.

There remains little now but to let the dogs in this book take over for themselves, and they can do this with very little help! Doubtless someone's favourite breed will have been missed out, but this is, unfortunately, inevitable. Somewhere a choice has to be made and we have tried to make that choice as varied and interesting as possible. We can only hope you

will feel that we have succeeded.

(LEFT & ABOVE)
Yorkshire Terriers (adult & pup). As its name implies, this member of the terrier family had its origins in Yorkshire. Because of its small size and lively, typically terrier-like, personality, it gains in popularity all the time as a game little family dog.

(ABOVE)
Dalmatian. For some time it was thought that the breed originated in Dalmatia, in Yugoslavia, but this theory has now been discounted. The Dalmatian was originally used as a companion dog, particularly on mail coaches, as it has a great fondness for horses and would run for miles under the carriage. Still a great companion, it is a dog that needs plenty of exercise to keep it happy and fit.

(RIGHT)
Saint Bernard pup.

Reggie
Smith

where they were kept, for many hundreds of years, as court dogs. They achieved a rather unfair reputation as 'lap-dogs' which was certainly no fault of their own as they are very lively little dogs.

(BELOW)
Alsatian. This, the famous German
Shepherd Dog, is surely the archetype dog
hero. The breed has been featured in
countless films since Rin-Tin-Tin. It not
only looks the part but has also proved its
real worth with police forces and the armed
services throughout the world. Although the
Alsatian is undoubtedly a powerful dog and
a very effective guard it is a deservedly
popular house dog, noted for its faithfulness
and lively intelligence.

(ABOVE)
Two lovely English Setters enjoying the
peace and quiet of an English country
garden.

(OVERLEAF)
Boxer and pups. The Boxer owes some part
of its breeding to the Bulldog, which is
readily apparent from its features.
Originally bred in Germany the Boxer is
now very popular in Britain perhaps partly
because, despite its boisterous nature it
makes a very good family dog and appears
to be particularly fond of children.

English Setter. A very 'English' dog, the
sort you would expect to see on a country
estate. They are a very old breed of dog
originating from the Spaniel with the
probable introduction of Pointer stock.

(ABOVE)
Saint Bernards.

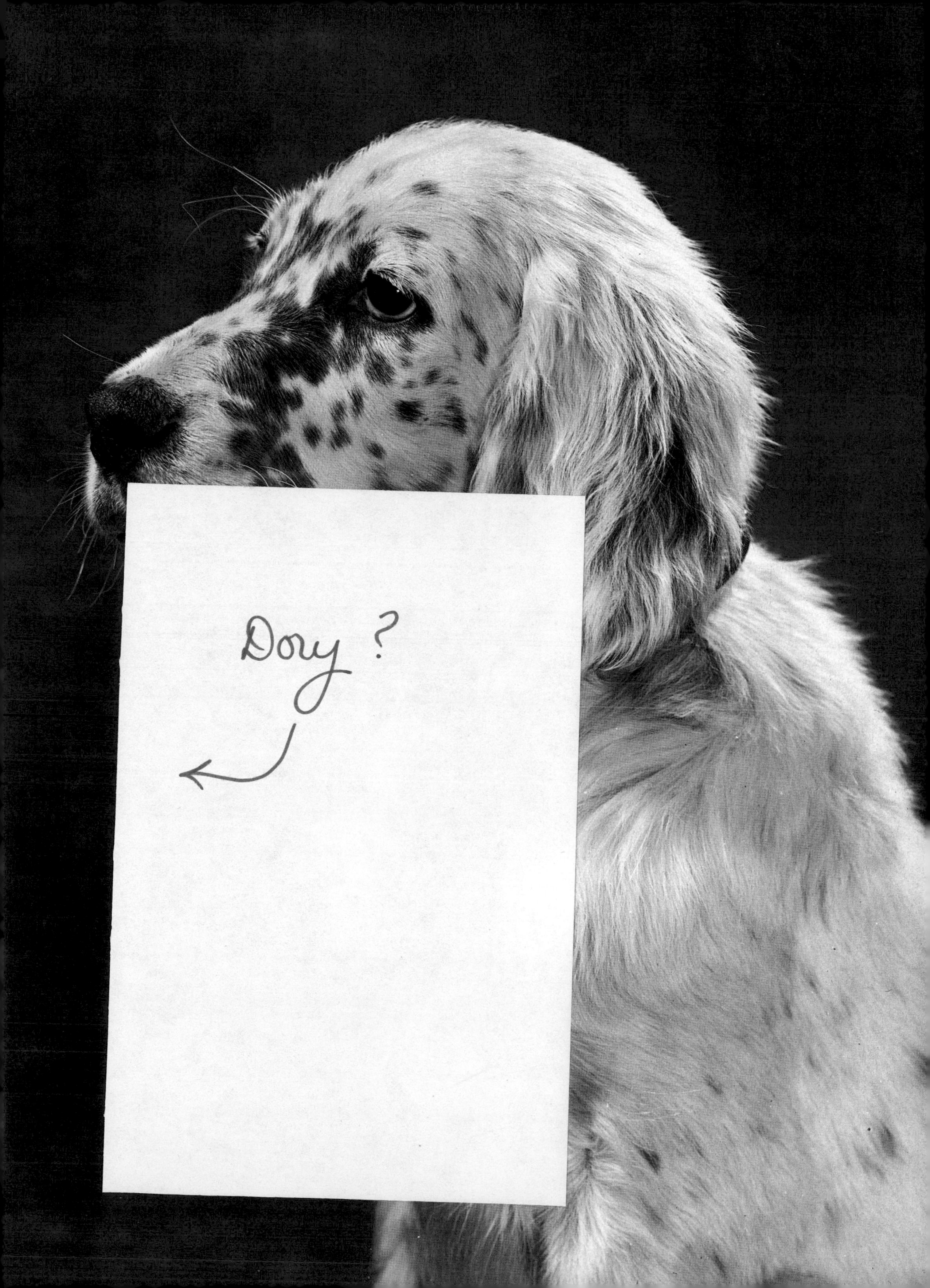
Dory ?

(BELOW)
West Highland Terrier. It seems strange to think that this lively and affectionate little dog was originally bred from the white (and therefore unwanted) puppies of Cairn Terriers! Now recognised as a breed in its own right it makes a very happy family pet.

Dina

(ABOVE)
Poodle. The cut, or trim, that adorns many of these bright dogs has a practical value. When they were used as water hounds it was necessary to trim away much of the hair to facilitate swimming. In order to protect their joints, however, long hair was left on parts of their legs and around the chest.

(ABOVE)
Collie. The Rough Collie, ('Lassie' to so many children who remember the films and stories of her exploits), originated in Scotland and has a long history of useful work as a sheepdog. It is a very dignified, highly intelligent dog and, properly groomed, has a quite magnificent appearance.

(LEFT)
Bloodhound. 1066 saw the arrival in England of the Bloodhound together with William the Conqueror. The dog was used primarily for hunting but its extraordinary ability to follow trails, sometimes days old, led to it being used as a tracking dog by the police and thereby to its association with less factual detectives, notably Sherlock Holmes.

(RIGHT)
Irish Setter. These very beautiful dogs were originally bred in Ireland as hunting dogs. The rich chestnut colour of the coat is an outstanding feature of the breed.

Chihuahua. This intelligent little dog which has a strongly developed hunting instinct for such a small animal, shares with much that comes from South America a mystery concerning its origin. Some consider that it was once the sacred dog of the Aztec Indians whilst others feel that it was probably roaming wild and was domesticated by the Indians. Although their size would prevent the possibility of them acting as a deterrent to intruders they are by no means lacking in courage and would certainly raise the alarm.

Enos
Cabell

(ABOVE)
Dachshunds (pups) Distinctively short legs for the length of the body and evidently the most distinctive characteristics of the breed. They make excellent little house dogs and they are usually very happy and affectionate although they lack the Basset Hound's traits of being rather disobedient.

(RIGHT)
Smooth-Haired Fox Terrier (pups) One of Britain's oldest breed of Terrier. The name Terrier comes from Terra — Earth, and this is exactly what this particular breed was used for digging foxes from their holes. They have also been very successful in shows, as well as making very lively and affectionate pets.

(OVERLEAF)
English Springer Spaniel pups.

(BELOW)
Cairn Terrier. A tough little dog named after the 'cairns'—heaps of stones—found in the Highlands of Scotland where the breed originated. The Cairn probably shares the same parentage as the Scottish, Skye and West Highland White terriers.

(RIGHT)
Old English Sheepdog. Also known as the 'Bobtail' due to its tail being entirely docked. The Old English Sheepdog is one of the most picturesque dogs with its long shaggy coat and its eyes normally completely hidden by hair. It is one of England's oldest breed of sheepdog and also makes an ideal family dog.

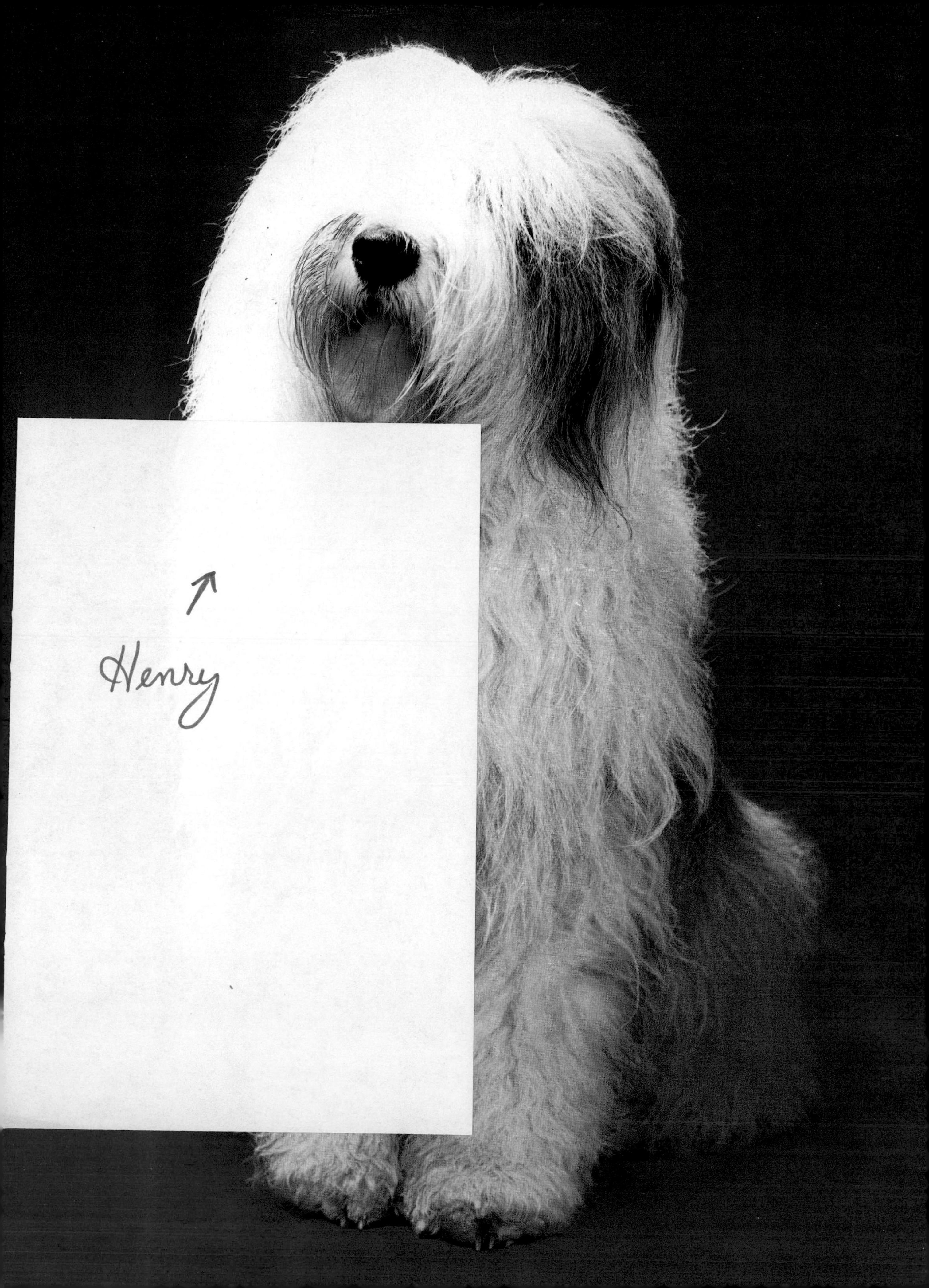
Henry

(ABOVE)
Shetland Sheepdogs. Both the Shetland pony and the Shetland Sheep are small animals and the Shetland Sheepdog continues this tradition. Bred as a working dog they are still used for this purpose although they are now more commonly found as pets and show dogs.

(LEFT)
Labrador Retriever. Because of its temperament, obedience and trustworthiness the Labrador is considered an ideal dog for training in the responsible job of guide dog for blind people. It seems that such a task is one of the highest attainments a dog can reach, and is one that this particular breed fulfils admirably.

(RIGHT)
Golden Retriever.

(TOP LEFT)
Welsh Springer Spaniel. Not long ago the
Welsh Springer Spaniel was rarely seen
outside its native Wales, where it was
probably introduced from Brittany. As with
all the Spaniel family it is very much a field
dog as well as making a very good
household pet.

(BELOW LEFT)
Bearded Collie. Originally thought to have
come from Poland, the Bearded Collie is by
no means common in Britain. It is probable
that the Old English Sheepdog owes at least
part of its ancestry to this breed.

(BELOW)
Cocker Spaniels. Spaniels always seem to
have a rather sad expression but they are, in
fact, very happy dogs. A very old English
breed, they were once used primarily as
gundogs but have now found great favour as
general family pets, for which their
temperament is ideally suited.

(OVERLEAF)
West Highland White Terrier pups.

(BELOW)
This particular illustration of young Basset
Hounds shows, to great effect, the long
trailing ears so characteristic of the breed.

(RIGHT)
Beagle pups. The Beagle is the smallest of
the hunting hounds and they may be seen at
almost any Hunt. Because of their size and
friendly nature they are popular as pets but
it should be remembered that they are real
hounds, and as such require quite a lot of
exercise.

(BELOW)
Poodle. An extremely popular house dog once used for hunting water game. Its abundantly thick and woolly coat has led to a great variety of haircutting techniques and shapes which tend to make the dog appear dandified; an appearance which is contrary to the true nature of the dog.

(ABOVE)
Two delightful little terrier pups, alert and very ready to get into mischief.

(TOP LEFT)
Corgi

(LEFT)
Basset Hound. When fully grown the Basset lends itself all too easily to caricature because of its general shape, the long body and very short legs contrasting oddly with the dignified head.

(OPPOSITE)
An intelligent and faithful little terrier of great courage, and not a little obstinacy! The Sealyham can trace its origins back to Captain John Edwards of Sealyham House in Pembrokeshire who, needing a small terrier to hunt and kill vermin, set about breeding such a dog. The result, the Sealyham terrier, is very popular, particularly in the United States.

(RIGHT AND BELOW)
The terms 'Cross-Breeds' or 'Mongrels' which can be applied to these alert and charming dogs, should not necessarily be thought of in a derogatory sense. Most breeds have been crossed at some time in their ancestry and if they are loved by their owners, and return this love, then nothing more needs to be said about their breeding.

*King Charles Spaniels. So named because
of King Charles I great fondness for the
breed and featured in many of the paintings
of the monarch, they are very much a
British dog and are seldom seen elsewhere.
There was, at one time, an attempt to
rename these affectionate dogs English Toy
Spaniels but this was abandoned and it is
still known by its original name.*